N[illegible]

To

Sunshine

PUBLISHED BY: Thea Evans

Copyright©2025 All rights reserved

No part of this publication may be copied, reproduced in any format, by any means, electronic, or otherwise, without prior consent from the copyright owner and publisher of this book.

Contents

Introduction

In the hidden chambers of pain, healing must be first for one's freedom for self, not to please others' opinions of comfort.

Hello, good people, my name is Thea Evans, welcome in as you follow along with me to briefly experience my life, maybe you can relate or understand. We have all had moments of pain, just on different streets and avenues. Some things here may bring up difficult emotions as you tune in, but that's okay, we are releasing them together this was difficult to process as I wrote. I'm glad I was obedient to God in getting this out; it was necessary to do this for the healing of others, not just myself.

Chapter One

Ugly scars can be beautiful

Imagine walking through the park late at night to get some fresh air which seemed like a great idea. The park is safe and peaceful, right? Then you begin walking into the park to realize things aren't as they appear. The first couple of steps you take feel so serene already, and you think this is a good idea. From a distance, you begin seeing beautiful sparkly glimmers throughout the park. This piques your excitement to see it up close moving swiftly to realize. Before encountering what allured to be amazing turned into horror. As the moment of how or why explodes in your mind, the sharp pain beneath you is agonizing. Afraid to look down the millions of shards of glass that once glimmered to the eye from a distance cuts you deep in many ways without warning. Who filled this beautiful park with broken glass. It's everywhere I don't think I can walk my feet are bleeding fragments of glass have pierced through my shoes. What kind of scene introduction is this to envision? Welcome to my beginning of how it all started I am not going to heed any warnings buckle up. During the end of summer in the nineties I was established and sent to such a place I had no idea about at least for now that was. Introduced to my parents who showed portions of love to an extent they believed was a good amount next to their habits of choice, to fathom life for themselves yet alluding to being figured out some way. My parents were in such a toxic environment not just a physical place this had shown up in every area of their lives. Born into chaos with the expectation to bring loads of peace to a situation out of my scope of support is what I presumed. Being the only child didn't last too long it was only momentarily before my baby brother came into the picture taking up space to fill as I had done. Understanding now we were born without intended plans in hopes to fill void depths. Yet that wasn't enough to prune their lives for the better. Assigned big responsibilities without developmental skills for life let's see how this turns out.

Chapter Two

Stolen innocence

Things changed my parents were no longer together but that hasn't changed their circumstances or drug use. Going to school was sometimes a vacation away from my mom's critical behavior towards me I became her emotional punching bag. I was already self-conscious

little one with many thoughts of trading my family for a better one. There were many moments I just knew I was adopted from the very start. My brother was my mom's favorite especially because I wanted to spend time with my dad when she became too difficult to stomach. Everything in my life was changing due to the weight of my mother's problems I began to bear on a daily. Exuding as the essence she dumped her problems on with her face full of tears I carried it as my mission to execute. Seeing my mother in another toxic relationship made things on the same level as death to me. When? I screamed from the inside of my aching heart as I clenched my chest wishing it was a dream. Seeing dysfunction once more expanded my desire to grow wings to just fly away. Moving day has proceeded once again certainly not wanting to start from scratch again. Can't she just get things right I pondered? Well, maybe this time she is going to be better and find peace; wishful thinking was the only hope I could fathom. My brother and I started going to a nice lady's house until my mom or her boyfriend got off work. She had kids as well, so we had others to play with while we waited. But I got tired of going there I wanted to go home after school sometimes, suddenly things had changed at the lady's house she would leave us there with her dad when she wanted to go to the store. As a little one I felt uncomfortable I didn't know her dad he seemed creepy and strange to me. One Friday afternoon I had to go over there I'm not sure where my brother was this day, but I was there without him. My mom's friend decided to head to the store and leave me with her dad was she setting me up I thought. As I sat there in hopes she was coming back soon, her father began saying very vulgar inappropriate things to the child of elementary age. He had such an ominous look in his eyes as he looked me up and down saying how sexy and beautiful I was. I immediately removed myself by heading to the restroom knowing something wasn't right with this picture. I went to pee thinking he would stop I looked up to see him coming inside of the restroom with me. I began to get up quickly he insisted that he should wipe me I then said it was ok he could leave I had things covered. At that point he began touching me with a huge grin on his face, then he started to reveal his manhood to me. I tried to leave the bathroom for the eightieth time then the front door made a loud noise as it did, he then allowed me to leave. I was disoriented why did this happen? Was it my fault? And why did my mother leave me to be hurt? This was the start of everything and everyone around that was once innocent to me I had to watch closely. I began to be nervously terrified of all things, especially men. In addition to now having a distrust towards my mother and her lack of discernment.

Chapter Three

Can you hear me

As a bit of time passed by, I started elementary school I guessed by now you think things have started to look up we shall see. Some things have Things changed my parents were no longer together but that hasn't changed their circumstances or drug use. Going to school was sometimes a vacation away from my mom's critical behavior towards me I became her emotional punching bag. I was already self-

conscious little one with many thoughts of trading my family for a better one. There were many moments I just knew I was adopted from the very start. My brother was my mom's favorite especially because I wanted to spend time with my dad when she became too difficult to stomach. Everything in my life was changing due to the weight of my mother's problems I began to bear on a daily. Exuding as the essence she dumped her problems on with her face full of tears I carried it as my mission to execute. Seeing my mother in another toxic relationship made things on the same level as death to me. When? I screamed from the inside of my aching heart as I clenched my chest wishing it was a dream. Seeing dysfunction once more expanded my desire to grow wings to just fly away. Moving day has proceeded once again certainly not wanting to start from scratch again. Can't she just get things right I pondered? Well, maybe this time she is going to be better and find peace; wishful thinking was the only hope I could fathom. My brother and I started going to a nice lady's house until my mom or her boyfriend got off work. She had kids as well, so we had others to play with while we waited. But I got tired of going there I wanted to go home after school sometimes, suddenly things had changed at the lady's house she would leave us there with her dad when she wanted to go to the store. As a little one I felt uncomfortable I didn't know her dad he seemed creepy and strange to me. One Friday afternoon I had to go over there

I'm not sure where my brother was this day, but I was there without him. My mom's friend decided to head to the store and leave me with her dad was she setting me up I thought. As I sat there in hopes she was coming back soon, her father began saying very vulgar inappropriate things to the child of elementary age. He had such an ominous look in his eyes as he looked me up and down saying how sexy and beautiful I was. I immediately removed myself by heading to the restroom knowing something wasn't right with this picture. I went to pee thinking he would stop I looked up to see him coming inside of the restroom with me. I began to get up quickly he insisted that he should wipe me I then said it was ok he could leave I had things covered. At that point he began touching me with a huge grin on his face, then he started to reveal his manhood to me. I tried to leave the bathroom for the eightieth time then the front door made a loud noise as it did, he then allowed me to leave. I was disoriented why did this happen? Was it my fault? And why did my mother leave me to

Awkard and feeling alone not knowing why I even exist in this moment as I pull myself to get aligned with my mother's next phase of movement. My voice has been stolen who will hear my silent sobs as I hold on to what was left of me? Just as things are gradually changing again, we are headed to my grandmother's house. My mom describes to my brother and me what is happening and where we are moving. We arrive to our journey's end worn out and hungry. My mother was a bit on edge as well as showing she was putting her best foot forward. Feeling that this was going to be an intense encounter my grandmother came out to greet us. She was so full of life and excitement as she embraced us so tightly with so much love. I wasn't sure of what change was upon us nevertheless I had no choice but to see. The next day we met our uncle who lived there as well he was different than most uncles in a not-so-friendly sort of way, he spoke but for the most part, we came and ruined his paradise from the looks we exchanged. The flow of things transitioned quite smoothly at first. The struggles of my mother had returned more so she just kept it hidden well. A new day arose as we registered for a brand-new school I wasn't looking forward to this at all. The children were advanced to the point life was experiencing them not the other way around, is this still elementary school I wondered. Some of the children were kind but most were vicious bullies even though mom was the first bully in my life. I learned much during this time a lot I wish I didn't know, and some were just weird facts to be determined. My mother made friends during this time of course with those who dabbled in the same struggles she possessed. Finding out along with other news of our unique family dynamic mom was pregnant with my baby sister. Grandma wasn't thrilled with the news. My little sister was born, in addition to now new arrangements had to be made. A significant time had passed my baby sister was now a toddler. Mom was back to her old self in no time. At this point, I began making threats to many of the people coming by the house for Mom. Standing at about four feet I felt as though I was seven feet tall trying to keep my mom safe, in a way of kicking her habit. Mom was so tired of me during this time I just couldn't allow her to be high in peace. I would locate her drug hiding spots and throw them away back then I didn't know how I knew where the spots were, but it was only God using me to help her. Things started to get normal except when Mom treated me like an enemy of the state. She was constantly mean and cruel to me for no reason as I tried to figure out what had I done to be treated in that manner. Grandma had to step in to check mom all the time because of the way she behaved towards me. I wasn't even allowed to sleep with her like my brother and sister, so I began sleeping with my grandmother. I was consistently rejected by my mom for being different than the others, or I was too sensitive and when I would state something was wrong, I was told I just wanted some attention. I was struggling even at that time with my mental health as a kid. Mom met a new friend who had a daughter a few years older than I was, and she encouraged me to begin hanging out with her. This girl was wild and had experience in many things children shouldn't be aware of. One day after school our moms left us while they went to run a few errands that seemed to last more than six hours. My mom's friend's daughter asked me about watching movies because she was bored, I agreed to watch not thinking she would put in a vhs porn tape. Disturbance began to fill my body, and I was scared all over again flashbacks of the incident that occurred in that bathroom. I left and immediately went home not caring if it was too dark to walk home. When Mom came home, she yelled at me for walking in the dark and not waiting on her, but there was no point in saying anything I already felt unsafe with her. Other moments came about I had been over to mom's friend's house her daughter was always excited when I came over. She pretended to be normal when her mom was there and once her mom left, she would discuss the most repulsive things. This one time I was over, and she said she wanted to show me something and decided to come out in lingerie. I was going to leave but my mom told me if I decided to pull that stunt again it was me and her; I didn't want that kind of drama with mom. So, at that moment I was stuck there waiting for my mom to come back. This girl was just as bad as the man who took advantage of me. She walked towards me and put music on to dance to in my mind I knew something was wrong with her. As I looked away to avoid her shenanigans, she began to touch me and grope me saying she was horny. I moved away telling her to stop I'm not comfortable she ignored what I expressed and put her hands in my shirt and pants. I told her to stop so she said just relax you will like it. Someone ended up knocking on the door, so she ran to the bathroom to put her clothes back on. Mom came back shortly afterward, and I was able to go home after that happened, I never went back there again.

Chapter Four

Welcomed in pain

Trying to understand why yet again I have become the target of violation by these sick monsters. I'm not feeling even safe around my mom at this point she has once again left me with people she didn't analyze first, I could've just blamed the drug use, but I despise excuses. Maneuvering as though everything was fine had become my new norm to suppress all things tough. Walking around on eggshells to stay out of my mother's way to keep her from using me as a punching bag of choice. Then later after her frustrations were out, she would cry to me about her problems as though I could handle them. My heart broke for my mother just to know how heavy things were. But I still couldn't dislike her fully because I loved her. Grandma was on top of Mama's head for it all I was trying to have moms back. But now I get why she did this as I got older to see my mother in different phases of time. This day I was learning how to cook I loved watching my grandmother cook so I was ready to begin. Now mom taught me a few things to start me off on my cooking adventure. I figured I fixate on a new hobby I liked karate among others, but I wasn't supported and was told it wasn't for me being that I was chubby, I heard that so many times so I began dieting too lose weight my mom had to know that would just strip my confidence so I just stopped trying to pursue things. Grandma was my mom she gave me wisdom on what I needed to know as a woman of integrity, I was taught that when leaving the house don't look thrown away. Grandma would tell me to make sure I always have on clean not raggedy panties in case of an emergency. She taught me to maintain my hygiene as well as learn proper life skills. She was a stand-up I'm about my business kind of woman very independent that's how she raised me to be in addition to a no-nonsense type of standard. When I first got my period mom was locked up and grandma was working, I was in such a panic not knowing what to do at the age of 9 a few days before my birthday what a happy birthday to me. The house phone began ringing and it was Mama I expressed to her what was happening she almost had a heart attack which didn't make my anxiety ease up any. Mom was always dramatic about all things even when it wasn't physically happening to her, she always made things concerning me about herself and made feel me invisible. I had to remind her, hey I'm here she told me to stay inside and call grandma. Here I was with such a heavy flow that initially lasted nine days why is all I could ask, but I felt alone and dirty reminding me of when I was taken advantage of. I made the phone call to Grandma at work she reassured me it was going to be ok she was coming but first she needed to buy me pads. So, I got in the shower, and by the time I was getting out Grandma was there with pads. She showed me how to place them and how many times I should change them along with washing up, all while feeling the most excruciating cramps that hit me like electric shocks from front to back. The cramps were so bad I would vomit I just didn't want to be me in that moment. Now it's a day before my birthday and grandma wants to have a small birthday get-together, I wanted to avoid it my period was on I was in pain and mom was in jail. I'm not sure if anyone would find this celebratory. Fast forward it turned out bad we were bored so we decided to go outside. The following day Grandma went to run some errands my little sister went along with Grandma. So, my brother and I decided to go out to play my uncle wasn't even there, so we took a risk. I told my brother we would lock the front door and keep the back door unlocked. After a while, we came back inside my uncle was back, and we feared what he might say. He came out of his room with an enraged look; he interrogated us I told him it was my idea. He beat me severely as though I was a man on the street, I had bruises everywhere my brother consoled me letting me know he would teach him a lesson for what he had done to me. I had revenge on my mind to end his life while he slept. That next week he kept losing money, but my brother was taking it to show him his payback, so my uncle was already on edge, so he started taking it out on us constantly. I can remember we were too loud once he made my brother, and I line up like in school and forcefully pushed us down into the tile floor on each other like we were a dead body pile. He choked me once almost until I was gone because I took a dirty top out of my little sister's mouth. But Grandma and Mama jumped on him to get off me. He walked around that house with such hate in his heart for us, we were living with a demon that was set out to destroy. One evening my uncle was working he was security at the airport checking the airplanes to ensure they were empty. A Maintenace guy was working on this plane my uncle was patrolling as well. As my uncle was headed out some way or another the guy closed the door on my uncle's hands, and he lost his portions of his fingers he was left with nubs. He called my grandmother he was so distraught, and everyone seemed to be concerned. My brother and I just sat there as my brother chuckled. About what happened I just knew God had served justice for how we had been mistreated.

Chapter Five

Big responsibilities

Middle school is presenting itself so quickly that I'm not even ready for it but hey here we go. I was going to the sixth grade this was quite intense didn't know what was ahead of me. The main things I was anticipating were whether I be bullied and is my hair would be cute. I thought the kids were something in elementary some of these kids were parents. There was this one girl in my class who already had two children and ended up getting pregnant as the year progressed. I went to school with a few cousins and some friends from the neighborhood which made things easier for me. Before I knew it, we formed a crew that extended the following year with my brother. My mom was trying to stay out of trouble, but she couldn't shake it off fully. By this time, I was learning more about responsibility as a big sister which eventually took place as a second mom because, at such a young age, I was a nurturer. Mom decided to move across from Grandma to take the initiative as an adult who could take care of us and herself. I was told when mom wasn't there, she depended on me to be a big sister to make sure my sister and brother were taken care of while she was out. I despised the idea of caring for them as though I created them why couldn't she just pay someone to do it? I was blessed early on with Godly wisdom and understanding to know what needed to be done. So, I treated my siblings like they were my children I still view them as my babies today. I was very overprotective and involved with their wellbeing I would even get on my mom's case about things. Growing up quickly and experiencing life even faster I felt like I was already forty in an eleven-year-olds body. I had no choice but to be mature and develop as this life that was dealt to me pushed for it. Even among my friends they would call me mama and ask for advice as I would nature while fussing at them. School was coming along somewhat smoothly I was figuring out who I was and who I wanted to be moving forward, and I was still in the process of finding my voice so I could protect myself. I started to realize my thoughts were a bit aggressive especially when it came to someone attempting to wrong me. I began noticing anger issues dwelling within. There were a few instances where a few kids decided to pick on me for not having what others had, which caused me to want to hurt them in ways that would have me jailed. Knowing that I would just keep it to myself unless someone upset me to the point of no return. Shifting ahead to the next phase of my life I was headed to high school which was one hardest moments of goodbye I had to face without any warning. Grandma and I planned a day to go shopping and stop to get some food. After shopping, we went to Golden Corral to eat. The day was so fun yet refreshing it was the day I could be a kid and enjoy some part of my life with my favorite person. As we drove home Grandma came across as weary, I asked her are you ok Grandma? She replied yes baby I'm ok just tired. My cousin was coming over for the weekend, so I just felt Grandma needed some rest we had a long day. I gave Grandma her meds and rubbed her back before heading to the bowling alley she went to sleep, and I left. I came home to some unfortunate news Grandma was rushed to the hospital she had a heart attack. At that very second, I felt my heart sink if only I was here I could've been there with her. I was just starting my first year of high school I

needed her. The next morning, we went to see Grandma she had to undergo surgery it was too much to process. Day in and day out we went to

visit, this time Grandma asked to speak to me alone. So, mama went out of the room I sat on the bed with Grandma she held my hand looked me in my eyes, and said don't leave your mom she needs you she can't do it by herself. When I heard that statement from my grandmother's mouth, I immediately thought to myself I'm trapped here. I talked a bit more with her I couldn't help but cry, she told me she was going home, and I was thinking she was coming home to us. Her room had been changed that same week. My sister was too young to visit so my brother stayed home with her, so it was my mom, my aunt, and my god sister. Everything looked great Grandma was up talking smiling and laughing, I knew this meant she was coming home soon with us. Grandma went back to sleep, and she had such a beautiful smile on her face. I left for a second to use the restroom that's when she took her last breath

Chapter Six

Unconditional love departed

Help!! Please someone reach for me I'm feeling numb this can't be real my grandma who is my mother figure, the one who I related to the most, the one who I look exactly alike is gone forever. God, I don't have anyone can I please have her back? Who's going to protect me who will love me unconditionally? Lost without any sort of understanding where do I put my emotions how will I adjust to this, I have no one to talk to or trust. Mom spoke to us briefly about what was going to happen next far as grandma's cremation memorial service, she also was putting my little sister in a grievance camp to process but what about my brother and me? I had to hold things together to be my mother's strength I was there in my head wondering how things will get done. Will be able to survive? Mom's drug addiction was still present it began getting worse as the days grew. The money that was gained after Grandma's departure was spent recklessly. My mom told us she was going to put money away for us to build interest in the form of a CD that was picked away until nothing was left. She was out even more than ever just partying only God knows what else was taking place. On this night our god sister was over, looking after us while mom went out for the night. My brother was irritating me so bad for some reason he decided to call me out of my name multiple times. I asked him kindly to just leave me alone and stop, but he wouldn't which caused me to have a blackout episode I had no clue my anger would be that severe. I just lost it and started spazzing my brother's eyes got so big he ran into the bathroom to hide from me I broke the bathroom door and took the door off the hinges. He ran so I went after him put his head through the closet door and hit him screaming at the top of my lungs. He ran outside to go over to his friend's house to get away from me my god sister tried to stop me, but she couldn't I was enraged I chose to go to bed and woke up in the middle of the night getting whooped by my mom for what I had done but did not say one word to my brother for calling me a fat bitch over and over. I was tired of her never supporting me or having my back. So, I made up my mind when I got a chance I would leave for good. Self-destruction was in full effect mom was spiraling out of control my brother and I just watched in disbelief and my little sister was too young to understand. My brother started giving up on everyone he lost his care for all things once grandma died. Grandma was gone mama's drug use got worse my uncle moved away and I had to step up as a parent for everyone.

Chapter Seven

Organized in the chaos

A game plan was in the works of my mind I had to get my family out of the lion's den we were going nowhere fast. I tried to get Mom to go back to school to further her education and better herself. I kept mentioning a fresh start would be great for the four of us of course mom would shoot down the idea. I was working overtime to get us packed up and far away from this place of despair. During this time, I experienced something else life had tossed, I went to the youth fair came home and woke up my eyelids very swollen as though someone had shoved cotton balls under each eyelid. Mom took me to the emergency room to find out what was going on. That was a complete disaster this crazy doctor tried to rub my eyes with a cotton swab, and I objected very boldly. So, there was an onset of doctors I ventured to see. We went to a specialist who set up an eyelid biopsy to understand how this occurred. Once the labs came back, I was diagnosed with the autoimmune disease Sarcoidosis. While processing all of this I was just trying to understand why this life had just become such a massive hardship. I sat in a second of what was happening, I never allowed it to steal the essence of my laughter. Eventually, Mom gave in to the idea of leaving. She called my aunt she came down to help us to push forward for the big move, there was going to be change for once I was hopeful. We moved to another state altogether leaving the ashes of rust behind trailing forward. Months have gone by my siblings, and I have adjusted to our new schools. Life was starting to feel a bit better on the surface. School was always a place that I just wanted to get over with. All I wanted was to get my diploma and move on my own to obtain stability in my life. Not expecting to make friends I met a girl in my homeroom class who was different just like me. We would talk all the time about our dreams and laugh about everything; she always brought big boxes of Cheez-Its and juice I just knew her mom shopped at Sam's Club. On a particular day where we would crack jokes and laugh this guy who sat with us decided to make jokes about us and when the joke was on him, he got so upset and called us out of our names. I felt so disrespected for the both of us and knocked him upside his head causing his glasses to come off. He wanted to fight so I picked up the desk I was ready to show him. From that day she and I became best friends; we have been best friends now for twenty-one years that was one of the greatest things that came out of that time. Skipping ahead Mom had been trying to stay clean and made a promise to me to be better she even gave me a ring to show her promise was holding weight. I believed her yet a bit apprehensive but willing to have faith in the situation itself what else did I have to lose? My birthday was sliding around the corner, and I was going to need a mini vacation. I was worn out mom was still getting high, and I was playing the role of a second mom to my siblings and my mom I was cooking, cleaning, helping with homework, washing clothes making sure baths were done getting them up for school stressed alongside caring such a heavy burden. I knew by my sixteenth birthday I was going to go for a visit and not come back an action I was willing to take to free myself. In making that decision some may say I was selfish but seems I was there to suffer and not get the nourishment I deserved. The words my grandmother said echoed in my head not to leave my mother she couldn't do it alone. Many of you would most likely judge me but either way, everyone will view it from any side, I didn't care my shoes were tailored to fit me to walk upon this journey.

Chapter Eight

Space to free

My birthday week had arrived my exit plan was nearing I was so ecstatic to be heading away soon to enjoy my childhood of what was left. I was all packed up making phone calls for my departure and arrival times. A short delay came into play, so I had to wait the following week to go it was ok I was still going. My god sister picked me up from the Amtrak station we went for food while reminiscing on old times it had been so refreshing. The piece of summer I got to experience was soon over and it was time for school again, my mom was calling to see when I was coming back home, I told her I was not coming back she cussed me out. So, my god sister spoke to my mom telling her I could finish school there and she would be responsible for me considering that she was completely older than I was mom agreed. I enrolled in an adult education school to get my diploma sticking to the stipulation for me to stay. I did what I set out to do I was motivated as the clock progressed my birthday was coming around again; I got a job as an event security. Not to mention my god sister did the same work as me so it was fun and something else in my life that gave me responsibility. I had my diploma and a fun job. Now I focused on hanging out and experiencing the nightlife. My god sister had me in clubs at the age of twelve, so it wasn't new to me. my age wasn't believed I had been top-heavy since fourth grade. I was experimenting with drinking hanging out late not having a care in the world only thing I wanted was to have fun and enjoy myself it didn't last long. I started to feel depressed not resting most nights in addition to getting bad headaches daily. Something was off but I couldn't put my finger on it exactly I knew I needed to call Mom. Once I called everything had become clear I had to go back to her I could feel the heaviness on the phone it caused me to weep so I returned to her house. Booked my ticket on the Amtrak and prepped myself for what was to come as the uncertainty of said situation made me quiver. I got there my siblings were happy to see me but were also upset that I had left them behind. Asking if I would leave again but I couldn’t give a definite answer. One’s mind could only imagine how things would soon go bad. Observing and not analyzing too much was my strategy to hold on. My mom's boyfriend was living with her he was a great guy just had a few issues, he considered us as his children he became a father figure our dads weren’t involved my brother and I dad was on drugs in and out of jail and so was my little sister's dad as well. I was going to the community college to further my education while being there. My brother and I began hanging out like we did as kids, my brother was my best friend we always argued and fought but don't let someone say something about either one of us just know it's us and you. The forward motion of the clock pulled everything into a decent space until I came home one day, and the house was torn up like in the movie scenes where the police ram shacks a house after serving a search warrant. I asked Mom what happened, and she was crying so I immediately sensed her boyfriend was the culprit of the madness. She expressed to me he hit her so I went to go get my brother so we could handle it. She begged me not to say anything but once my little sister saw it all my brother was not going to calm down. My brother left after hours of seeing the boyfriend wasn't going to show up. Her boyfriend came back in a rage wanting to still fight so I had my hammer to defend my mom, and he pulled out this huge Samari-looking knife on me. I could feel myself about to black out I was angry I was going in and out then I looked him right in his eyes and told him to use it I know you didn’t pull it out for show. He came back as though he wasn’t within himself, and he ran out of the back door I wasn’t afraid of what he would do, but I was so angry with my mom for tolerating it all I know this hadn't been the first time. I called my brother on the phone to discuss what happened, he was on his way quickly. I told my mom he must leave he cannot come back here. She yelled at me you do not determine who leaves my house this is my house. I was hurt by the words piercing in my heart but not surprised, so I replied what I would determine was my leaving. I booked my Amtrak ticket to move back in with my god sister. As the clock rolled in the time for me to go Mom asked could she and her boyfriend take me to say their goodbyes and he wanted to apologize. I agreed to accept the apology and for them to accompany me, but I was crushed inside by her choosing this man over her child. She cried so hard as I parted the train to leave but not one once of me was a bit moved by it. Call me cold but I endured enough disappointment at the hands of my mother.

Chapter Nine

Why did I show up

Once again heartbreak was my portion to bear, I just didn't want to even be around her again. Before then I already felt like an orphan I was alone. Not being understood by anyone around. One would start to question numerous times why am I even here anymore? what's the purpose? Since the time I can remember I wanted to be a part of another family with both parents and less disfunction. Or better yet why did my mother have me? Being away from my siblings was hard for me daily but I knew after we talked about me leaving the last time, they would never forgive me again. A significant amount of time had passed I was still living with my god sister constantly clubbing and drinking, including hanging with other friends who did the same but twice as much. I also enrolled myself in cosmetology school to start somewhere with a career I was undecided about what I wanted so this is where my start began. I received a call from my mom that week to my surprise she called to let me know she was moving back so we could be near one another my little sister would come with her, but my brother would come sometime later she even apologized for what took place with her boyfriend. I heard her but I didn't get why this was even a thing a bit confused I just went into details about where they would live among other minor details. Formulating a blueprint for the next phase of life knowing my mom was coming back was she going to be a better parent or was this to drop my guard my heart was soft yet bruised. I was a bit stressed after hearing the news not knowing how things would turn out. Was she sorry for what took place or was this a temporary band-aid for the real bruise coming? As the clock passed remnants of time the day had arrived mom was here to live again, putting my best foot forward expecting better that seemed to be my point expectations. Mom ended up going to jail for an old charge my sister was living with her godmother until mom got out. I had to get her school supplies and clothes the new school year was coming her godmother acted as though she didn't have it, but she was the one responsible for my sister. Forwarding fast Mom was looking for a place to move and I was moving with her, so she made me give her half of the deposit money to move in even though she suggested I move with her. Her new boyfriend was moving in, and I asked where his money was to put in, I got cussed out, so I left it alone. This was my first time meeting him and I tried to give him a chance. Not knowing he was another one who liked putting his hands on women. I received a call from my god-sister that mom was in the hospital with a huge knot on her head. Mom lied she stated she fell later down the line I found out he caused the knot. We ended up moving to another place where mom had her heart set on the prices were more affordable. Yes, her boyfriend was still around this time I had to buy my sister's bed my bed, and other things for the new place. I was beyond livid once again she had me do these things and her boyfriend didn't help he was a broke boy. I didn't respect him at all how could you not help a woman you're with let alone put your hands on her? I would hang out all night cause problems drink every day I wasn't concerned about being responsible because at some point when could I have fun and not have to take care of anyone not even myself at that point. Partying consistently being promiscuous just not loving myself filled with anger and malice in my heart. I was so angry with my mom for the way she treated me, the people who sexually violated me, and anyone who disrespected me. I would wake up angry ready to explode waiting for the second to erupt with raft. going around with an I don't care mentality and murderous thoughts. It got so bad I invited a guy over to sleep in the same room my sister slept in I don't know what I was thinking but looking back who was I something was completely wrong within. My anger began to get worse as the days progressed a walking volcano erupting at any moment. My mom and I got into a heated argument I bawled up my fist and hit the dining room table, so hard screws popped out Mom yelled you better not tear up my table as she left for work. Still fuming in rage, I picked up a chair to throw it, to my surprise my sister and godsister were standing in the corner protecting each other feeling I was going to hurt them, so I stopped. Deciding to have a conversation with my mom about the violation I endured, not expecting much but I was going to see how this played out. Allowing her in about the first situation was very dismaying she didn't embrace me, ask me the important details about how I felt, or anything. She got on the phone to find out if the guy was still around, I get that, but I was standing there in need of my mother. After that day my sister woke up early in the morning before school and decided to write a hate letter for the house. She stated she hated mom's boyfriend, and she hoped he died, that mom gets on her nerves and dislikes her sometimes, finally, she hated me because I was mean, and she would stab me, but she was too afraid of what I might do to her. Mom called my sister's godmother over so we could have an intervention for her. I was past the conversation I want ed to fight since she wanted to stab me. Intervention time came she was yelling, and I was jumping over the couch to get her. My sister's god mom was trying to calm me down mom's boyfriend was outside upset, and mom was stressed. Things eventually came back down to what was considered normal my sister apologized to everyone but stated she still didn't like mom's boyfriend which I understood.

Chapter Ten

Losing to win

Through the sequence of life, I did have one person in my life who was my first love we first met and became friends he was there for a lot of the chaos. Our bond was toxic yet loving in so many words. It was short-lived his life was taken away from him at the age of twenty, I felt my heart was snatched out of my chest the night I received this heartbreaking information from his sister after seeing it all over social media. I then watched the news confirming this again I was in such disbelief I couldn't feel or hear anything around me he was gone. With pieces of progressing grief in my heart, I was depressed I didn't want to leave my room for anything. My friends were at the house constantly there supporting me through it all. Every time I slept, I would dream of him so I would sleep just to see him, mom thought I wanted to be with him it was just a severe pain in my heart that echoed so loudly that everyone near heard it. My friends would bring me out into the living room to watch TV and I would just cry hearing certain music play. One day I decided to go to church with mom and my little sister, my friends came along as well they were my team we were there for one another often. At church that morning I was able to get a breakthrough from my depression that day thank God. I started going to church after that day, I was thinking about getting my life on track finally. All things started shifting in my life I celebrated my twenty-first birthday at the club with drinks for the last time. I gave up drinking, partying everything toxic in nature. Next, I was working on my anger I was sick of myself and asked God to give me a new heart the old one was damaged beyond repair. This Sunday was different I got a prophesy about new beginnings taking place in my life soon, and I was looking forward to it. Before realizing things started taking off in my life for the better, I got a new job I was feeling better. Right when I decided love wasn't for me after such heartbreak, I met this guy that I immediately connected with there were fireworks between us. We fell for one another swiftly I knew it was right in my heart. He was such the perfect gentleman always considering me, taking me on dates. I was sharing new experiences in life I could picture this man being my husband. We went to church together he would spend time with my family we all got along well everyone loved him. He took me on a date he planned for us it was so beautiful I was so intrigued by the essence of how he loved me. At that very moment he got down on one knee and proposed to me with a temporary ring, of course, I said yes. I was twenty-one he was twenty-two we decided to tell our parents when we were ready. But it didn't go as planned we took my sister with us to look at some rings and she told my mom we were engaged. Mom was so angry with me for not telling her I didn't feel it was a big deal because I had never seen her genuinely happy for me with anything. I was already making plans to leave her home because I knew things would get worse after she wasn't included. So, moving day came we moved in together and were married by the next month on his birthday our birthdays were two weeks apart so that month was very special for us. Mom didn't come to the courthouse neither did his parents when we tied the knot, we prepared to not have support. Everyone felt it was too soon we were married after six months of being together. I get the concerns at the same time I didn't care this was our life to live out. Married life was amazing until it wasn't so many objections to our union werc cxpressed daily it weighed down on us heavily. There was war between both our families seemed like the Romeo and Juliet story. As the journey continued, I saw how there was a strong dislike towards me from his mom she disapproved of me greatly. I knew it was more of a control tactic because she was losing some of the say-so in his life, he was a momma's boy who depended on her for everything until he met me. Our marriage trailed forward at about the fourth year he cheated on me and became very disrespectful I was begging God to remove me from this agony. Time went on we moved out of state he still was such a trifling individual I didn't know him anymore; I was worn out from mothering and defending him. It got to a complete point of no return for me when he left and had a baby with another woman. At times I wasn't the best wife I would cuss him out and belittle him for his actions and for not being the man I needed to lead. Mom called one day letting me know she was moving away, and we should come to visit so we did. It was a bit of a road trip, but it was needed I was depressed and giving up on it all. This marriage had become a tug of war in real life not to mention I gained over sixty pounds food became my device when things were too tough. We enjoyed the new scenery so much that moving there was the next phase. There had already been a disconnect between us I wasn't even being intimate with my husband anymore I just knew this was going to be our last time together. A discussion was had, and I decided to end things because he wouldn't stop cheating and God had presented me with my answer, I was partially free from this he acted so shocked that I mentioned a divorce like he was the victim of all sorts of mistreatment. I was over him and ready to restart my life. He packed his things and moved back home with his parents I still loved him as a person but on to getting back to me was necessary.

Chapter Eleven

Moving on

Scooting into the next phases of what felt like movie clips of my life jump-started again. I no longer had a husband I was with Mom helping with things and staying out of her way. She didn't want me to leave but I just couldn't leave I terminated my lease, so I had to hurry up and find something. Working down at the hotel as a housekeeper wasn't ideal but very interesting I and a team of others helped to open a new hotel. Before getting the doors of the hotel open, we encountered wild coworkers a drunk, a few liars, a thief, and someone who was doing incantations. Right out of a movie, this was work

I knew who would do what and I saw them do exactly what I imagined. Of course, those people ended up being fired or quitting especially when the head chef of the kitchen stole pots, pans, and the hotel's projector I said several times he was up to no good. Yet some of it was entertaining but the motto I live by is "I don't get involved" so I didn't. I came across some cool people I hung out with outside of work for the most part we became great friends. Heading home from a long day of cleaning twenty-seven rooms I wanted to take a hot shower and see my bed. Dragging up the stairs the neighbor's son decided to speak, and I just stared at him as he smiled, I said don't talk to me went inside, and slammed the door. The next day came I saw him again he said good morning I replied yeah to him and headed to work. Day in and out he would speak I would just ignore him and keep going about my business. Mom was looking for a new place to move she was going to allow me to keep her old apartment, and I just switched everything over in my name. She got approved for the new place but didn't have time to pack due to her busy work schedule. I volunteered without her knowing I got boxes and packed all her things for her. She came home from work to see everything was ready for moving day I completed the task I was ready for her to go so I could enjoy the quietness. Mom was a loud person in addition to always bothering me about something. I couldn't handle loud noises and chaos it was very triggering for me with the kind of environment I grew up in. My coworker who I had become friends with asked her husband to help assist mom in moving some of the smaller items to the new house. The bigger items were going to be moved by my uncle the next day he had a truck to move the rest. As moving day arose Mom was outside talking to the neighbor, she was such a sweet lady that I later adored, she was the mom of the guy who spoke to me all the time. I went outside to speak; the son came out he appeared different from the last time I saw him or maybe I just never noticed before. He was a big guy standing at about six foot four three hundred and thirty pounds very solid he was a giant to me I was only five foot three. I was intrigued but still not budging to converse with him. I had a bag of trash in my hand his mother stopped me from taking it out she instructed him to do so I said thank you then proceeded to go get more trash from upstairs. I sat down for a second to watch one of my favorite shows on the Cooking Network. I hear the front door open and it's him smiling rubbing his hands together. So, I ignored him to continue tuning in to my show he cleared his throat to introduce himself while rubbing his hands together. I replied before he could finish "Look I know your name already you met me before “You know mine now stop rubbing those hands are you trying to start a fire? I know they're dry. He replied you're feisty I like that. I pointed to the direction of where the trash was, so he laughed and took it out I did say thank you.

Chapter Twelve

Curious enough to try

I stopped working at the hotel not long after this due to my kneecap bone started moving out of place. As I allowed it to be healed, I got a job at the local hospital as a housekeeper this was a whole new experience of upkeep. This was the first week of orientation and learning so many rules and policies for the job. A lot of note taking with long videos so this was the easiest part. I was planning on going home after work to clean up, shower, and then order some food. Mom came to pick me up from work and take me home we had to go get a few things from the grocery store. As we pulled up to the apartment complex I got out of the car and went to grab my things out. The neighbor's son was in his car he jumped out offering to help and my mom said don't be rude let him help. I just moved to the side as he grabbed the bags walking me upstairs, he stood at the door I told him to come inside to take the bags into the kitchen. He was a bit nervous not so smooth today I noticed. We had a really good conversation he even vacuumed my floor and took out the trash as I washed three bowls in the sink. I thanked him for helping me and I told him I was going to take a shower, and he could come back to continue our talk. He was surprised I told him I needed your number how will you know to come back he stumbled a little that I was straightforward. Right after I showered and put on my pj's I let him know to come back upstairs. He came back and sat on the couch across from me which was fine it showed he had respect for me not all in my personal space. The conversations we shared were very engaging yet refreshing while talking to him I sensed that he had a past with drugs, so I asked he admitted to that being in his past. I didn't judge knowing we all come from different walks of life who was I to make him feel ashamed. We talked more until it was late thanked God, I was off so I could rest being up this late. Before the night ended, I told him whoever you're talking to tell them you are taken now. He got his phone out so quickly and did just that, I told him I was joking he said oh no I'm your man now. The next morning before I could open my eyes, I heard my phone singing it was a good morning text followed by a call for me to get up and get ready. I got up to prepare myself for the day not aware of where I was headed. I headed downstairs to his house his mom opened the door with a great big smile. She was always so pleasant and sweet to me I just loved her, the first thing that came out of her mouth was I'm so happy my son told me y'all are together now. She began celebrating our newfound love story things just started last night it was funny to me. As she and I were talking he walked up smiling saying wow baby you look very beautiful. His mom said yes, she does with those big baby doll eyes if it was possible, you could see me blushing. We headed out to run a few errands and he picked up some things for my house as well. I didn't expect that, but I appreciated his kind gesture. Once we got done, we went back to my house, and he decided to order food for us while we watched a few movies until we fell asleep. The next morning, I got ready for work he wanted to take me and bring me lunch. The day was close to over he texted me and stated he was off work and could pick me up. We headed back to the apartment he went to help his mom around the house, while I went to rest until he was finished. Mom invited me to go to church with her I agreed to do so I had been once before I enjoyed going the move of God surely was there. The first time I went there I met this wonderful woman who is now my loving aunt who I talk to daily. I also met the overseer of the church she was the woman of God who was in charge when meeting her it was like meeting a part of myself, I had to learn. She is also still in my life; she became my godmother whenever things are happening, she's one of the first to call me. I continued going to the church and even joined. My spiritual walk with God was important to me, I needed to stay grounded despite my mishaps during the journey.

Chapter Thirteen

Love that covers a multitude od sin

Passing through the beauty of love aligned with what I wanted but soon faded into dark uncertainty. My relationship was full of intense passion; we loved one another so hard that it hurt. We became codependent, and it wasn't healthy at all. We were two broken children trying to fill voids only God could fill. He started using it again. I didn’t leave. I loved him and tried my hardest to get him help. A part of me felt like this was something I wanted to do for both my parents, who struggled the same. Aiding him made me think I was helping my dad, who was still in that lifestyle. I truly loved him, I couldn't abandon him, my life advanced in such a rocky way. Relocating to another place of convenience was best to keep a hold on the bills, he couldn't keep a job, and everything was falling on me to uphold I was so angry yet embarrassed like being a kid all over again. His mom was dealing with serious health issues that kept us over at her house quite often to look after her to make sure she was ok. A lot of times we just stayed there in case she was in need due to staying across town it was easier to be close by. Progressing to the next she wasn't getting any better as the days neared to something least expected. She told me that it made her so happy to have me as her daughter-in-law that she was giving me her blessing, even if she wasn't here to witness when we would get married. Mom and I, along with some of our family, were preparing to go on a cruise soon, but I couldn't think about going, considering his mom had been in the hospital as we slept there day after day. Kidney failure had been the culprit of this whole ordeal. His mom was a strong woman who had been fighting this for some time now. In my heart, I knew she was tired and ready to go; there was no convincing her to stay awhile longer, she had already written her letter to heaven for release. One night, while sleeping at the hospital, I had a dream that she would go soon. That dream shook me up as I woke. The nurses informed us to be present; his mom had a stroke in addition to having a heart attack, and she could no longer speak. I didn't cry to be strong for him as he leaned on me for his support, it was very trying to hold him without knowing what to say, so I just gave my presence, wrapped in love. The doctors came in to inform us to call everyone because she didn't have much longer left. Bad news had come in, flooding us heavily. The room was filled with screams and sobs. Regretting the day of the cruise came I didn't want to leave him I was horrified he would overdose.

Chapter Fourteen

The world has crumbled

The funeral happened, and we were picking up the pieces slowly. My boyfriend decided to go to rehab. I was hopeful for his change of pace, but deep down I didn't believe he was quite ready for change; nevertheless, supported him anyhow. He went and completed the program, which didn't last long enough for an adequate treatment that was needed. I asked him to stay longer for better results; he assured me he was well enough. Mom came by the house to check on us as well. She informed us she would be moving out of town to be closer to my nephew and my niece. Soon after I noticed something had been off with my health, I figured my iron was low, so I should start taking my iron supplements again. I was tired, not to mention I was experiencing a massive flow of a menstrual cycle with huge clots that were shaped very oddly, and the pain I felt was so unbearable, I'd never seen or experienced such a thing like this before in my life. A little over a week later, I went to the hospital several times, only to be sent home without finding out anything. At least until

Sunday morning at three o'clock, I tried to get out of bed to pee, but I couldn't walk because of extreme pain coming from my flank area. I screamed so loud it woke my boyfriend up he rushed to me as I cried. I can't walk, so he carried me to the bathroom. He ran to grab his phone to dial 911. This indeed was past an emergency. I was in the hospital trying to understand why and what. The doctor came into my room. His exact words were Call Mom so she can be here. I can't let you go home. A bit confused, asking why what was wrong, he then replied from your labs, you are in stage four kidney failure. There was no way this was possible. How could this be happening to me? I felt I was being punished, and death was coming for me. I was only twenty-nine. Mom came down to be there for me. The doctor had no way of explaining how this came to be, so I had to get a kidney biopsy done. Afterward, my doctor concluded my Sarcoidosis was the villain of kidney failure, and I was born with a small right kidney that never grew and just stopped working. Fast forward, Mom wasn't going to leave me there with my boyfriend, so I had to pack up and leave him. We both sobbed like babies. My heart was shattered, and I had to leave him. That wasn't the only heartbreaking situation. I was still bleeding, not knowing I had miscarried. It had been forty-five days of nonstop bleeding. I went to the hospital, and my mom met me there after work. I asked the nurse not to mention it around my mom; I didn't want to be judged. I had to get a blood transfusion and a dilation and curettage; going through this without him was hard.

Chapter Fifteen

Family or Foe

A whole year passed I was on dialysis. By this time, I was over this process, even living at this point. Away from my boyfriend, was in jail finishing his probation time since he decided to mess up when I left. Feeling deeply that this was punishment for something I had done, as helpless as I could be, my best friend and my auntie wouldn't allow me to drown in this. I just wanted peace, which was very hard to receive. My best friend prayed with me daily, assuring God was centered throughout my situation. Living with Mom wasn't easy, especially as I expected me from her which had been my problem quite often. Mom or my siblings didn't offer to give me a kidney, my heart was in pieces. I said to myself, everyone had made an excuse, implying their kidneys were probably bad. If that was true, they would be in my shoes; they were going to let me die, I knew that to be true from Mom's response to me. Coming from the doctor. I was so upset after the visit, and I asked why no one had checked on me or come to see me. This is the moment mom told me, that just because you're sick doesn't mean everyone has to stop their lives for me. As she proceeded to bring up my ex-husband and my current boyfriend, I was already in a place where I was tolerated, so this was the icing on the cake. Beat down on your depressed, suicidal daughter who no longer wanted to live. My mental health was in a tormented state; I was going to be on the show snapped if I had to be here any longer. I wanted to express to my mom what was going on with me, but she did not try to understand me. She had rejected me for as long as I could remember. But foolishly, I stuck around hoping she would be a loving mother to me and change. I was stupid to keep trying when dirt was kicked in my face every time. I was screaming out for peace, understanding, and justice. I was desperately looking for a place to remove myself from the chaos. My niece's birthday party came, and I didn't attend, so my mom told my brother I didn't come because I was depressed that I didn't have my place. So, I wasn't able to see the kids. I started back praying, begging God for a way out. After praying, I had a dream about where to go. I then made a call to set up some arrangements to leave. My god sister helped me find a place near her, but it was far from my family, so I left to get a fresh start.

Chapter Sixteen

A jump down

Living in a new state was rejuvenating for me. I was determined to put my best foot forward. Managing my health was a priority, and next on the list was my mind. God had placed it in my heart to start therapy; I was a bit apprehensive but willing. Every morning, waking up was like enduring war. I would constantly have panic attacks my body was breaking down. I searched for a therapist to get myself back, it wasn't easy, who was I really without all the trauma attached, but I was willing to find out. My boyfriend was getting out, and my mom was willing to pay for his plane ticket. Her concern was me living alone without the proper help. I was fine living alone yet wanting him near was ideal. He was finally here; I was elated just to be able to hold his hand. Things were starting to pick up with us somewhat, I sensed that he had been untrue before coming home to me. I had a dream about the encounter with him and another woman; he was not forthcoming with the truth. I got quiet, and he spoke, telling me it was true. As my heart broke into tiny pieces, I jumped up in such a rage, I wanted to harm him, but I had to consider my health first and not go to jail. From that day forward, he was going to feel what I felt. I stopped talking to him as much. I didn't consider him in my life anymore. I was breaking away from him, and he had no clue but knew something had changed between us. I found a therapist to guide me in sorting out my life. I was diagnosed with the very things I knew I had as a kid: anxiety, depression, and PTSD. My therapist recommended I start taking meds to combat my symptoms, and to help along the way. Taking them for three months made me so nonchalant and zoned out; I hated the feeling. Those close to me could tell I wasn't myself, and my boyfriend made things worse by treating me as though I were a lunatic. The more I addressed myself in therapy, I saw that the only reason I was with him was that he reminded me of growing up, so it was time to release him. I was no longer in bed with dysfunctional, toxic behavior; I was empowered to heal and grow. I had expressed to him when getting home that evening big change was on the rise. He raised his head as he looked at me, trying to understand what I meant.

Chapter Seventeen

I can't believe this

The next day, we talked, and he did not agree with what I had to say. He tried to convince me he would do better. Considering I was already not in the relationship for a while now, nor would I allow him to have access to me. I was disgusted by the thought of him touching me, yuck. I wanted him to leave my life and never look back. He pleaded with me for us to work things out. He was using again and sleeping around with multiple women, thinking I didn't know. He became obsessed with me, stating that if he couldn't have me, no one else would. One night, he provoked me until I had a blackout, and I didn't recall what happened. When I came to, he was dragging me across the floor and began choking me, saying we would both die that night. As I was gasping for air, his nose was bloody, and his chest was cut up. I called the police nothing was done. He manipulated them into not arresting him. When I came home from dialysis the next day, he wanted to apologize, but I was too numb to hear or speak. I wasn't present within my body. That night in the bathroom, he wanted to talk, and I told him to leave me alone. He stood right in front of me, keeping me from leaving. I lifted my hand to scratch my head, he then slapped me, apologizing, saying it was a reflex, so I grabbed the disinfectant spray on the counter, snatched his glasses off, and sprayed his eyes. Oh, I was determined to blind him as he screamed in terror, calling me everything but a child of God. He tried to trap me in the bathroom while he washed his eyes out. Making it to the front door, he grabbed me, then I started to have a panic attack. He wouldn't just leave peacefully in his mind, I was going to be his even after I told him we were through, the love was gone. Winter was approaching again; he was higher than ever coming home, losing his mind. I should've known I would be the reason his frustration exploded. He yelled and argued, saying foul things to me. It bothered him that I wasn't afraid of his antics, so he then pulled a gun out on me and threatened to take my life and his own. Another police report was made nothing was done. It was that time of the year again for the holidays. I was still in therapy and working on myself while trying to get him away from me. I stepped outside for a moment, seeing him with another woman walk upstairs to the abandoned apt. I went upstairs, and opened the door, seeing him in action with this woman as he was begging every night for my love again. I was not going to let up or fall for his scheme. I was still processing who this man was because this was a stranger, not the man I once loved. He never treated me this way before, we had been together for almost five years. Everything he was dragging me through was still a shock to me. At that very moment, I went back into the house to throw his things outside. He called the police on me, saying I chased him with a knife, but I was sitting on the couch, very calm after cleaning the floor because he poured all my juice from the fridge on the floor. He lied, stating he was in fear for his life, so I was put in handcuffs. As the police took me outside, he then said she didn't chase me. The officer said it was too late; I had to go.

Chapter Eighteen

Life or death

My family pulled together to bail me out. I was missing my dialysis treatment. All of this had gotten further than I could fathom. I don't understand how I got to such a place. I was out and had a ninety-day protection order to stay away from him, or I would go back to jail. I got home to see he left, at least I thought so. I took a shower and got in bed with my face covered in tears, being depressed, I just wanted to leave and go away forever, I wanted God to take me from there. I got up at five in the morning, my usual dialysis hour, to call my nurse to explain why I missed treatment. Going back to sleep, I was startled by the noise in the living room. To my surprise, the crazy man broke into my house and greeted me with a tight embrace and a warm tone. He said I cleaned the house for you and made breakfast, you were resting so peacefully, I didn't want to wake you. This was a lifetime movie in real life, he acted as though nothing happened. I had to plan my escape from him. I couldn't go too far because I had to report that I was in the city every Tuesday and Thursday until my court date. I walked around pretending I cared for an individual I hated, knowing that if I showed any opposition against him, he would have me put back in jail. He decided to leave. I was relieved, but it wasn’t far from over. He had men watching my house, he would stalk me when I left the house, calling, asking who this was and that person I spoke with. He even camped in the abandoned apt next door to me; he knew the maintenance guy, so he had access to do as he pleased. When I would take phone calls, he would stand outside listening in the br,eezeway near my bedroom window. On this day, I tried staying away from home to avoid seeing him. As soon as I made it home, he came into the building right behind me, coming inside as I unlocked the front door. I wasn’t prepared for what was about to happen. He said I need you to sit down. I want to talk, I'm sure you don’t want to hear me out, but listen. I wouldn't reply, just nodded my head. He went on a rant about me disrespecting him, and he knows he hasn't been the best man to me, and he knows I want to leave. But did I think I was going to love him to the extent that I had and be with someone else, he wasn't going to allow it, as he stated. He then proceeded to tell me my love was something he would never allow someone else to have or get a chance to see, he would kill them. I tried to record him to protect me if the cops were contacted, so I would be clear in the protection order guidelines. But he said Leave your phone alone, I'm talking. I got up to assure him I was listening and walked towards the bathroom door he was blocking the bedroom door. So, I said can we finish this conversation after my shower I was sweaty and wasn't feeling well. He agreed and then changed his mind quickly saying you are trying to ignore me I'm expressing my heart to you bitch and you don't even care. Thinking to myself, this man is going to try and kill me, the way he spoke this had to be premeditated. He walked over to me and punched me in the face repeatedly, cussing and yelling at the top of his lungs. I begged him to stop as he said to me with his eyes pitch black, I'm going to drown you. All I could do was pull against him from dragging me into the bathroom, praying God was going to intervene. He let me fall on the floor. I ran into the closet, sobbing. He came into the closet, choking me with one hand, and punching me with the other. I could just feel my face swelling and bruised. I couldn't breathe, so he urged me to go into the bathroom to allow the steam to open my airway. I refused because I knew he would put me underwater if I did. Was my life about to end at the hands of someone I once loved dearly? While lying on the floor, I called out for Jesus to save me silently to myself. I was too weak to stand he picked me up and placed me on the bed I was so confused. I looked up at him, his eyes turned back brown, and I was praying he was done and was going to leave. Instead, he was crying and sobbing, he started apologizing for what he had done to me, asking for forgiveness.

Chapter Nineteen

Choosing to continue on

Regretting ever allowing such a person in my life was my fault and a mess to clean. I prayed and asked God to remove all hate and malice in my heart for this man. Being held down by brokenness and bitterness wasn't the story to live. I choose life outside of the chaos again, using my pieces of pain as a source to keep going. I had never allowed myself to grieve the loss of relationships with the ones who failed me time and time again, the time was now. My therapist would encourage me to sit in things to feel and not check out, as I often did. She would say Stop putting expectations on people, you will be disappointed, and everyone is not going to have the heart you do. As I released everything, I managed to obtain the peace that surpasses all understanding for once in my life. Still going to therapy, doing the work was still of importance to my growth and healing. Knowing my court date would soon come, I was a nervous wreck pleading with God not to allow me to be placed back in jail, and how sorry I was for staying in a relationship he didn't stamp. I was focused on doing what was needed to better myself daily. My ex was still contacting me, no matter how many times I blocked him. He was arrested at some point for whatever wrongs he had committed against others. I know it was God's way of pulling me out so I could leave without having resistance. He called me from jail pleading and begging me not to leave his life, and he would do better. I hung up the phone and never looked back. I was choosing for myself this time something that had never been done. I was determined never to allow my joy or peace to be stolen. You would think, as much as I smiled and laughed, my life was simple. As complex as life has been since day one, I have always found a way to smile. My scars, inside and out, reminded me of the strength God granted me to walk such a path. The judge dismissed my case. I could breathe now, my chance to live again without fear hanging over me as I slept. I prepared my mind, body, and spirit to exit a place that once appeared as comfort, no more excuses, just actions of moving forward. My new motto for life is glowing and growing. This is something I still work on today.

_ **Dedication**

I would like to dedicate this to my amazing support team. Being there encouraged me to move forward in completing this book. I was nervous about it, not feeling I could do it, but your kind words, in addition to sound advice, daily inspired me a great deal. I love you.

Made in the USA
Columbia, SC
18 June 2025

59544642R00043